KU-301-352

THIS BOOK BELONGS TO:

....

....

CONTENTS

First published in the UK in 2006 by Templar Publishing,
an imprint of The Templar Company plc,
Pippbrook Mill, London Road, Dorking, Surrey RH4 1JE, UK.

Illustrations copyright © 2006 by Douglas Carrel.
Text and design copyright © 2006 by The Templar Company plc.
Designed by Jonathan Lambert & Nghiem Ta.
Dragonology™ is a trademark of The Templar Company plc.
All Rights Reserved.
ISBN-13: 978-1-84011-715-8
ISBN-10: 1-84011-715-X
1 3 5 7 9 10 8 6 4 2
Manufactured in China.

templar publishing

www.dragonology.com

Dr. Ernest Drake's

Dragonology™

TRACKING & TAMING DRAGONS.

A GUIDE FOR BEGINNERS.

EDITED BY

DUGALD A. STEER, B.A. (Brist), S.A.S.D.

ILLUSTRATED.

THE TEMPLAR COMPANY:

PUBLISHERS OF RARE & UNUSUAL BOOKS.

*"Keep a lookout for obvious signs
of recent dragon activity."*

AN INTRODUCTION TO DRAGON CRAFT.

—◇—

"Where can *I* find dragons?" is such a common refrain these days that it seems to crop up almost every time our favourite flying beasts are mentioned. It often gives rise to the counter-question, "But what would you do with them if you found them?" Bearing both of these questions in mind, the intrepid experts at the *Secret and Ancient Society of Dragonologists* [S.A.S.D.] decided to commission a brief guide which would cover the essentials of practical dragon craft in order to answer them as thoroughly and succinctly as possible, and *Tracking and Taming Dragons* was the result. The book starts with the wise advice that the best way to begin tracking dragons is to keep a lookout for the more obvious signs of recent dragon activity. It contains a veritable treasure hoard of useful information that will allow students to quickly progress with their tracking skills, and also to gain a useful working knowledge of the best methods of taming these wonderful creatures.

Ernest Drake

STARTING OUT.

Newcomers to dragon tracking are often surprised to find that they do not need to purchase an array of expensive equipment in order to pursue this interesting pastime. A stout pair of boots or shoes and appropriate clothes for the season and location are all that are required in order to begin, coupled with a keen pair of eyes, an intelligent, curious disposition and an eagerness to learn. Of course, when a dragon is located, caution should be your watchword until a sense of trust has been built up.

WHERE TO START TRACKING.
Until you become an expert, it is best to search for dragon tracks where they are likely to stand out.

* *In jungle and woodland, tracks may be most easily seen in the soft mud or sand by stream or river banks.*

* *In snowy areas, dragon tracks are likely to be fresh, as they will be quickly covered by each new snowfall.*

* *Sand dunes can be a particularly good place to begin searching in desert regions, unless it is windy.*

COMPARING DRAGON TRACKS.

Each species of dragon leaves their own tell-tale footprint which can help the student to quickly identify which sort of species has been discovered. This is useful in making a risk-assessment of how safe it may be to approach any particular given specimen.

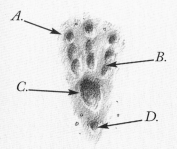

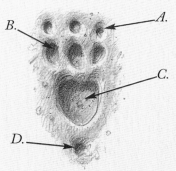

KNUCKER TRACKS.
A. Fairly light marks left by dragon's foreclaws.
B. Long, thin toe marks.
C. Small deep pad mark.
D. Prominent hind claw.

EUROPEAN TRACKS.
A. Deep, round holes left by long foreclaws.
B. Wide toe marks.
C. Wide, shallow pad mark.
D. Prominent hind claw.

9

Dragon Habitats.

Having a working knowledge of the different types of dragon habitat will enable the tracker to predict which kinds of dragons he is most likely to encounter. This can help enormously in the search as the tracker can then assess possible lair sites, and other places that are likely to be frequented by dragons, such as the edges of streams or mountain peaks, and begin scanning them for tracks and other signs such as scat [dragon droppings].

MOUNTAIN.

In the West, hunt for caves among the higher tops; in the East, pay attention to areas around streams, lakes and waterfalls.

TYPES OF DRAGON—European [*draco occidentalis magnus*]; Chinese *Lung* [*draco orientalis magnus*]. TRACKS—May lead to lair or cave of European dragon, or favourite water source of *lung*. SCAT—Large, smelly scat containing bones of prey [European]. No one has recorded *Lung* scat.

Indonesian Lung *footprint.*

Lung *dragon.*

European *dragon.*

European dragon scat.

10

DESERT & SAVANNA.

A camel may be quite useful in following tracks in the desert. While tracking in the savanna, be careful to avoid being ambushed by lions.

TYPES OF DRAGON—Wyvern [*draco africanus*]; Lindworm [*draco serpentalis*]. TRACKS—Wyverns often leave their footprints in sandy areas; Lindworm tracks are usually obliterated by their own tails. SCAT—Large, containing remnants of prey [Wyvern]; long and thin [Lindworm].

Wyvern scat.

Wyvern.

Wyvern footprint.

ICY REGIONS.

IN Arctic and Antarctic regions beset by frequent blizzards, the tracker may only have a few hours before tracks disappear forever.

TYPE OF DRAGON—Frost [*draco occidentalis maritimus*]. TRACKS—Frost dragon tracks remain visible until new snow falls. SCAT—Fresh frost dragon scat is quite warm and, in Antarctic regions, quickly becomes adopted by groups of Emperor penguins seeking warmth.

Frost dragon.

Frost dragon scat.

Frost dragon footprint.

JUNGLE.

PERHAPS the most difficult place to track dragons, due to its dense undergrowth and the likelihood of stubbing one's toe on Mex scat.

TYPE OF DRAGON—Amphithere [*draco americanus mex*].
TRACKS—The Mexican Amphithere [often known as the *amphiptere*] leaves snake-like tracks with its legless torso.
SCAT—Soft and squishy when fresh, amphithere scat soon hardens to a stone-like consistency.

Mex scat.

Amphithere.

Mex tracks.

OUTBACK.

RATHER than track dragons in the outback, one effective method is to lure them to you by baiting natural features of the landscape.

TYPE OF DRAGON—Marsupial [*draco marsupialis*].
TRACKS—Due to the infrequency of rain in the Australian interior, marsupial tracks can be hard to age as they last so long. SCAT—The temperature of a dragon's scat is the best way to tell how recently the owner was last present.

Marsupial scat.

Marsupial.

Marsupial footprints.

An ability to blend in with the natural environment so that the tracker becomes almost invisible may be a life saver.

WOODLAND.

HUNT for knuckers in the early morning. They are often found breakfasting near rabbit warrens, or waiting by the side of lonely paths.

TYPE OF DRAGON—Knucker [*draco troglodytes*]. TRACKS—Knucker tracks are best sought in the mud or sand by the banks of streams or ponds. They are particularly hard to see in leaf mould. SCAT—Knucker scat has the appearance of large but irregularly sized horse droppings.

Knucker.

Knucker scat.

Knucker footprints.

Tracking Techniques.

While a practised eye is the best tool in tracking dragons, there are a number of other tools that can be useful. Chief among these, and very easy to make at home, is a tracking stick, which can help you to find even the faintest impressions made by a dragon's feet.

A TRACKING STICK.

Take a straight branch, somewhat longer than the stride of the dragon you are tracking. From a clear set of tracks mark the stick as shown in the diagram below. In order to use it, place point A or B in the right place on the last visible set of tracks, and rotate the stick, looking for the tiniest signs. The next print must have fallen near the end of the stick.

A tray of modelling clay or putty can be placed on any path used by dragons to record footprints.

Tie twine markers at A and B to indicate the length of the footprint.

C.

B.

A.

A to B: Size of footprint.
B to C: Size of stride.
A to C: Size of step interval.

14

PLASTER CASTS.

In order to take a plaster cast of a footprint, firstly mix plaster-of-paris with water. Make a wooden form and press it into the ground around the print. Finally, pour in the plaster, and wait until it has dried before removing it.

a. Prepare the form.

b. Pour in plaster.

c. Remove the cast.

A TRACKING PLATE.

Take a flat metal sheet and hold it over a candle flame until it is blackened all over with soot. Next, place the sheet where you suspect that dragons—or other creatures—may pass by. Leave the sheet for a few hours. If you are lucky, you will see dragon tracks on it when you return.

OTHER SIGNS OF DRAGON ACTIVITY.

* Long, deep scratches on trees and rocks used to sharpen claws.
* Bones of animals that have been torn limb from limb.
* Abandoned villages burned in terrible fits of rage.

15

OTHER ANIMAL TRACKS.

Even though it can be particularly interesting tracking dragons, the experienced tracker is sure to come across a range of different types of footprint that have been left by other wild animals and birds. It can be useful to also be able to identify these, even if only to eliminate them as not having been made by a dragon.

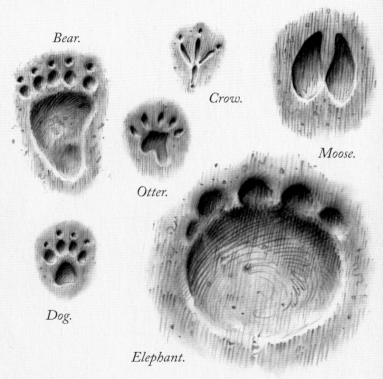

Bear.

Crow.

Moose.

Otter.

Dog.

Elephant.

A TRACKING CAMP

On expeditions that last several days, always remember to build your camp as far away as possible from the trails used by dragons. Remember: it is you who is supposed to be doing the tracking and sneaking up, not the dragon.

ADVANCED TRACKING EQUIPMENT.

Once upon a time the only gadget available to the master dragon tracker was a Dragon Ear Trumpet Helmet that allowed sounds to be discerned over huge distances, modern dragonologists may take advantage of a whole range of more modern scientific paraphernalia that has now become available.

DRAGON ATTRACTOR [pumps out the scent of the dung of a female on heat].

DRAGON HORN [makes a roar like a rival dragon].

DRAGON'S DELIGHT [makes a "baa" like a lost lamb].

DRAGON DETECTOR [with dragon dust, which heats up if any are about].

∗All of these items of equipment may be ordered, hired or purchased from a reputable dragonological outfitter.

17

APPROACHING WILD DRAGONS.

After mastering the art of following dragon tracks, it can be frustrating if, at the end of them, you find the dragon took to the skies and flew away. However, if you do find a dragon at the end, remember to approach it with care.

One useful method of approaching dragons involves the use of a dragon dummy costume, such as the one shown on the left. Be sure that your actions mimic those of a real dragon, or your encounter may be brought to a fiery end.

S.A.S.D. NOTE.

While the tracking techniques outlined in this book may be practised by anyone, the techniques outlined in the rest of the book are provided for information only. Make sure that you catch or train a dragon only in cases of actual need.

Remember, FATALITIES often occur as a result of young, inexperienced dragonologists being too keen to introduce themselves too soon!

HOW TO CATCH DRAGONS.

Although in the past, it was normal for western people to see almost all dragons as "problems" that needed to be "eliminated", nowadays a dragon that is a threat to humans, say by devouring them too frequently, can be easily caught in a simple dragon trap and then relocated.

Provided the dragon is hungry enough no great level of sophistication is required in trap design.

LOBSTER POT TRAPS.

One form of trap is called the "lobster pot." It is made of toughened steel mesh with a neck that allows inquisitive dragons in much more readily than it lets them out again.

LEARNING TO TRAIN DRAGONS.

It may come as a surprise to find that young dragons are no more difficult to train than big cats such as lions and tigers, although they can still prove highly dangerous to the uncautious. However, the training of adult dragons—which needs to be done more often, is a far harder task.

TRAINING BABY DRAGONS.

There is a chance that a dragon chick that you have hatched yourself will take you for its parent, and copy you in the same way it would its mother. There is also a chance this will not happen, and that the chick will be merely biding its time, waiting for a chance to get you.

TRAINING ADULT DRAGONS.

Adult dragons, particularly old, wise specimens that can talk, will resist all forms of training or dominance. Unless you can outwit the dragon, it is likely that a fatality—either your own or that of the dragon—is almost certain to result, along with all the attendant unpleasantness.

DRAGON TRAINING EQUIPMENT.

Apart from the whip—which is quite pointless as it will not hurt the dragon, but will rather enrage it—the items below are all part of the stock-in-trade of the modern dragon trainer.

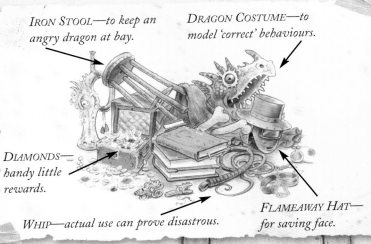

Iron Stool—to keep an angry dragon at bay.

Dragon Costume—to model 'correct' behaviours.

Diamonds—handy little rewards.

Whip—actual use can prove disastrous.

Flameaway Hat—for saving face.

A SECURE REFUGE.

Remember it is essential to have somewhere secure to keep your dragon when it is not being trained. Some dragons can find training sessions rather trying, and will be keen to demonstrate their anger.

Let the dragon calm down before resuming training.

MISTREATMENT OF DRAGONS.

All dragonologists must ardently seek out and expose cases of dragon mistreatment. Report all incidences of any activities such as those described below.

A Dancing Dragon. Tied to a stake, the poor beast is forced to "dance" for public amusement.

Hoop-La. Seen at circuses, the dragon is made to fly in and out of a fiery hoop, to the applause of the crowd.

Room Guarding. Some wicked dragonologists train captured dragons to fiercely guard their bedrooms.

This circus master learned all too soon the dangers of putting his head into a trained dragon's mouth.

GOOD REASONS TO TRAIN DRAGONS.

It is acceptable to train a dragon which needs to be moved from one place to another for its own safety, or to train a youngster you are raising in order to prevent unfortunate disasters. Here are some example commands:

Fly! A dragon that is learning to fly may be taught to carry someone on its back.

Fetch! A dragon that has been relocated may be taught to "fetch" its own treasure to its new lair.

Lie Down! This will assist in your hiding the dragon, should this be needed.

Roll Over! Useful for preparing the ground for your camp *en route* to the dragon's new home.

Die for the Queen! Not likely to be used very often.

A Training Regime.

Training must be regular if it is to be effective. You must be firm in your attitude. If you have decided to offer a dragon treats only when it performs some act you have trained it to do, it will be counterproductive if you then give it a treat merely because it "makes eyes" at you.

STARTING OUT.

As with all animal training, it is important to remember that at first you should not bother too much about getting exact results. Indeed, at first, almost any results will do. You may find, when starting to train a dragon—say, by performing an action you hope it will copy, and offering it a treat if it does so—that merely reaching a position where the dragon does not attack you too viciously makes a very good start. You may then gradually become more demanding

Expect repeated maulings—especially during the early stages of a dragon's training.

REWARDS NOT PUNISHMENTS.

It is worth emphasising that a dragon must be trained by a system of offering rewards for good behaviour, rather than meting out punishments for bad behaviour. As dragons learn by example, you will find that a dragon you have treated well will treat you well in return, while one you have severely punished can become quite difficult.

If a dragon disobeys you say, "No!" and make a firm gesture with your hand. It is, however, best to do this wearing crocodile skin gloves.

PERFECTING YOUR TECHNIQUE.

If you manage to survive the dark days of early dragon training reasonably unscathed, then you will almost certainly have earned a good deal of respect from the dragon involved. This bond—which grows firmer over time—will enable you to train your dragon to happily perform exactly those actions that you require of it.

DRAGON TRAINING CASE STUDIES:
PHINEAS FEEK'S FREAK FAIR.

These case studies show examples where dragons have had to be either rescued from wicked trainers, or trained so as to be moved. The first one concerns an American "Freak Fair" that starred not only dragons but a host of other magical creatures. Any dragonologist would have been horrified to witness the deeds Feek performed in the supposed name of "entertainment." I decided to put a stop to them at once.

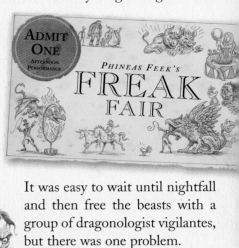

It was easy to wait until nightfall and then free the beasts with a group of dragonologist vigilantes, but there was one problem.

The dragon was so used to performing for Feek that it had forgotten how to hunt. It had also forgotten how to breathe fire. A short training session resulted in the dragon being ready for release. And, after a short "reunion" with Feek, it flew happily away to begin its new life in the mountains.

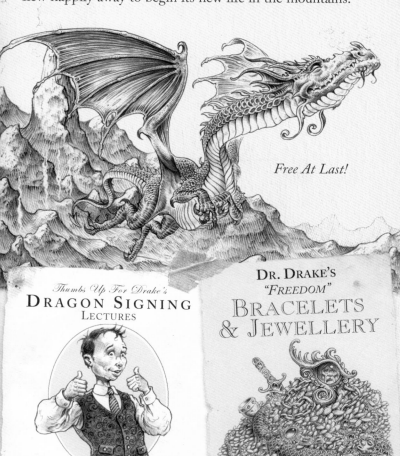

Free At Last!

Dragon Training Case Studies: Operation Flame.

In Operation Flame a dragon who lived too near to human habitations had to be moved for its [and their] safety. While the usual method would have been to retrain the dragon, this time speed was of the essence.

"OPERATION FLAME!"
DRAGON RELOCATION
from LOCH LOMOND *to* SKYE

For details on other relocation projects, please contact Dr. Ernest Drake at *The Dragon Kennels*, Pippbrook Mill, Dorking

The essence of the problem was that a dragon had taken up residence near Loch Lomond in Scotland. This loch lies near Glasgow [in terms of the distance a dragon can fly] and so it soon began to cause a problem for the local populace.

Expeditions were quickly mooted to kill the dragon. Fortunately, the Secret and Ancient Society of Dragonologists were informed, and the dragon was quickly captured and moved to the southern slopes of Ben Nevis. There, it was convinced of the benefits of moving to the more remote Cuillin Mountains on the Island of Skye. Seeing the benefit of this, the dragon itself transported a crack team of dragonologists to the island, and soon settled down in its new home.

S.A.D

"SAVE ALL DRAGONS!"

Ernest Drake

YOU CAN HELP!

S.A.D. Headquarters at...
Dr. Drake's Dragonalia, Wyvern Way, London,

APPENDIX I.

DRAGON WHISPERING.

A "dragon whisperer" has a great affinity with dragons, and often uses ancient rhymes to help with training. Despite being quite hard to understand—and almost nonsensical at times—they can be highly efficacious.

CALMING

What is louder than a stone?
And faster than a snail?
Lives longer than a mayfly?
Is wider than a nail?
What flies farther than a dog?
Is blunter than a sword?
Is fierier than water?
And has a treasure hoard?

Answer: a dragon

ROUSING

Dragons rise and dragons roar,
Dragons, dragons at the door.
Dragons flap and dragons fly,
Dragons, dragons passing by.
Dragons come and dragons go,
Dragons, dragons don't say no.
Dragons here and dragons there,
Dragons, dragons everywhere.

WARNING

I told you once, I told you twice
I told you once again
You said you could, you said you would
Not do the thing again.
I tell you no, I tell you, Go!
Don't let it be in vain!

BEFRIENDING

Draco-raco draco-rac,
Treasure's leisure's pleasure,
Draco-raco draco-drac,
Pleasure's treasure's leisure,
Draco-raco raco-drac,
Leisure's pleasure's treasure,
Aco-draco aco-drac,
Treasure's pleasure's leisure!

SUMMONING

Come forth scaly beast,
Come forth and feast.
Come forth and roar,
Come to my door.
Come forth and fly,
Come forth and cry.
Come forth and play,
But come forth today!

PUTTING TO SLEEP

Go to sleep my wyvern,
Close your weary eyes,
Fall asleep so deeply deep
Give in to sleepy sighs.

Go to sleep my wyvern,
Rest your weary head,
Lay it down with not a frown
Upon your treasure bed.

31

Appendix II.
A Tracking Journal.

The experienced dragon tracker is always careful to keep notes of his tracking experiences. Below you can see a sample page from such a journal—on the next page there is a blank version that you may copy to use yourself.

Dragon:	Wyvern
Date:	15th September 1875
Place:	Box Hill, Dorking
Age:	10 years
Size:	20ft

FIRST SIGHTING:	On the steep escarpment to the south of the main hill.
ACTIVITY:	Digging up flints.
TRACK MARKS:	
OTHER SIGNS OF DRAGON ACTIVITY:	Many trees have been burned or torn up. Usual signs of scat. An egg.

OTHER NOTES:

What a remarkable tracking experience! I was only expecting to find a knucker, but a young wyvern has arrived at Box Hill in Surrey and seems fascinated with digging up flints. He has brought an egg with him [his brother or sister?] He has torn up half a hillside so far. I must find out more!

APPENDIX II.
MY TRACKING JOURNAL.

Start your journal by making a sketch
of a dragon you have tracked.

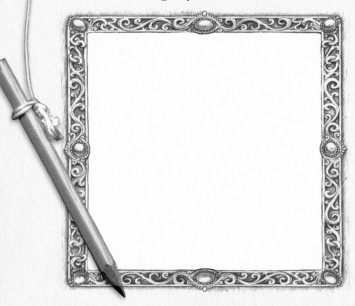

DRAGON: ....

DATE: ....

PLACE: ....

AGE: ....

SIZE:

From *Tracking and Taming Dragons* by Dr. Ernest Drake.

FIRST SIGHTING:

ACTIVITY:

TRACK MARKS:

OTHER SIGNS OF
DRAGON ACTIVITY:

OTHER NOTES:

Afterword.

Remember that, while tracking dragons is an enjoyable pursuit that can teach you a great deal about these noble creatures, taming them is another matter. As ever, I feel compelled to remind all students of dragonology that their main goal must remain the conservation and protection, not only of dragons, but of all the magnificent creatures of the earth.

Ernest Drake